Venus Flytraps

by Kris Bonnell

Venus flytraps are plants.
They have leaves.

3

4

A set of two leaves is called a trap. A trap has six hairs inside of it.

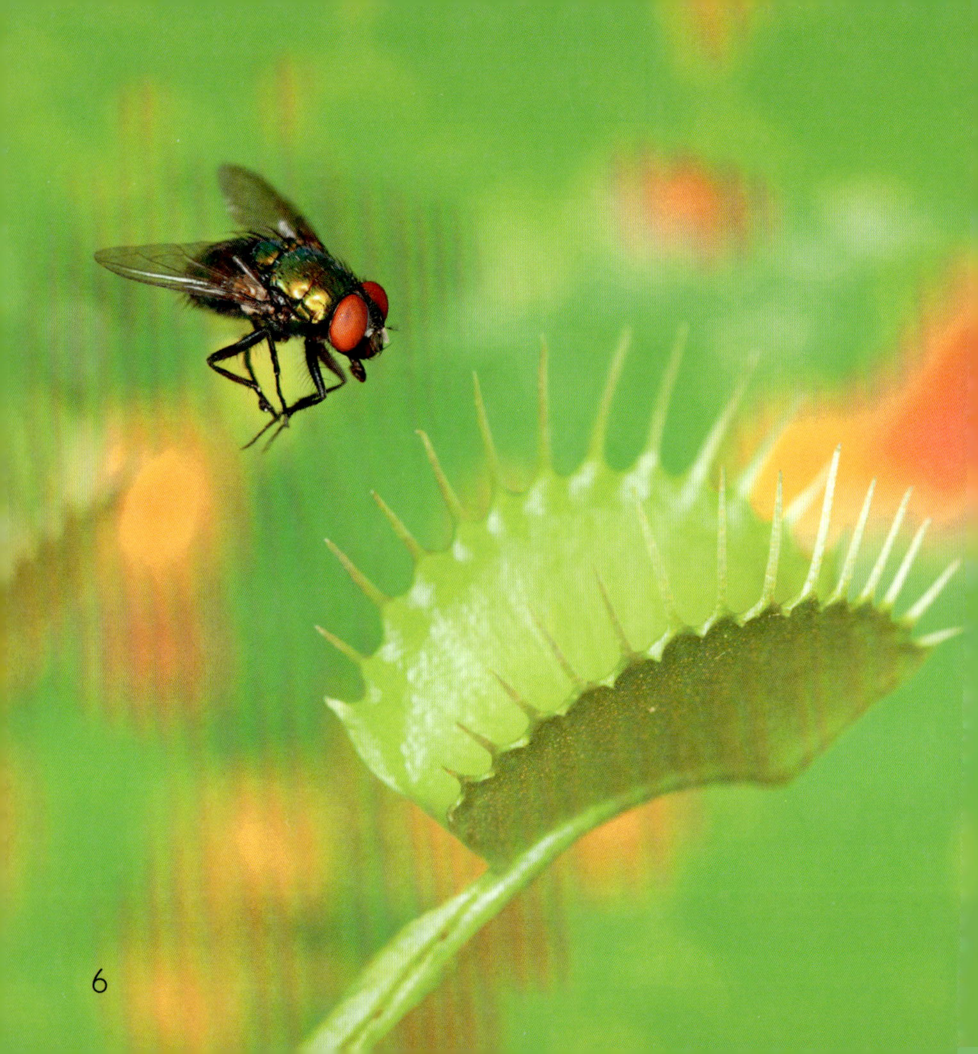

Flies like the smell of Venus flytraps.

Sometimes flies land in a trap.
If they bump the hairs,
the trap will...

9

SNAP!

Venus flytraps catch flies.

11

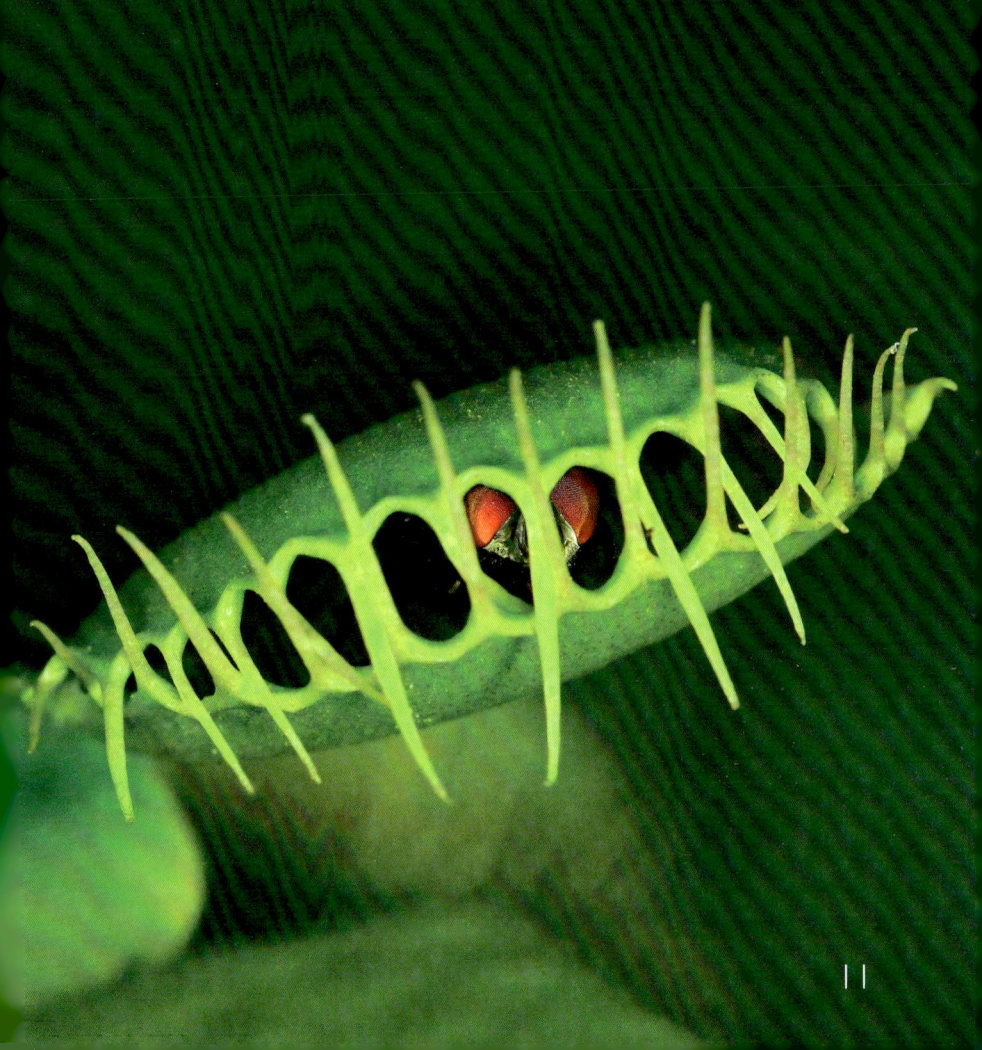

Venus flytraps eat flies!